There is Purpose in Your Valley

Other Books by

Dr. Arlene Kearns Dowdy:

A Poetic Love (2015)

Tales of Eastwood (2014)

The Delbert and Sarah Jackson Story, A Family History (2012)

My Mother, a Virtuous Woman (2008)

Website:

http://www.glotutoringandpublishing.com

There is Purpose in Your Valley

Understanding Life's Struggles

Dr. Arlene Kearns Dowdy

GLO Publishing, LLC
Willingboro, NJ, USA

THERE IS PURPOSE IN YOUR VALLEY

Copyright ©2015 Dr. Arlene Kearns Dowdy. All rights reserved.

No part of this book may be reproduced by any means, graphic, electronic, or mechanical, including photocopying, recording, taping or by any information storage retrieval system without the written permission of the author, except in the case of brief quotations with full citations.

GLO books may be ordered through booksellers or bulk orders may be fulfilled by contacting:

GLO Publishing, http://www.glotutoringandpublishing.com
GLOInc2015@gmail.com
1-609-871-1340

Because of the transitory nature of the Internet, any web addresses or links contained in this book may have changed since publication and may no longer be valid.

All scripture references are taken from the Authorized King James Version, unless otherwise noted.

All images are property of the author and may not be copied or used without crediting the author's full name.

ISBN: 978-0-9722269-0-5, Digital Edition
ISBN: 978-0-9722269-1-2, Print Edition

0972226915

REL 012040, REL 012070, REL 02120, REL 077000

Library of Congress Control Number: 2015912549

Printed in the United States of America.
GLO Publishing pub date: August 2015

For my parents, Lillian Ruth and the late James Franklin Kearns, who raised me in God's Word with love and prayer; my spiritual parents who have encouraged and spoken into my life since I was a child, Evangelists Perry and Ethelrine Hester and Dr. Gladys Long.

In memory of my national choir mother, the late Evangelist Ernestine Shiver, and church mothers, Mother Ida Ledbetter, National Mother Alice Curry and District Mother Lila Mae Clegg, all inspirational examples of excellence, beauty, strength, undying faithfulness, and love.

Photo 1: A Wadi (Valley) in the country of Oman

Contents

Introduction 1

PART ONE: TRIBULATION 3

Tribulation is Definite 9
Tribulations are Necessary 15
Reason for the Season 19
Let Go of Your Old Way 41
God's Way for Us 45

PART TWO: THE VALLEY 63

God of the Valley 65
The Valley of Vision 77
God's Anger in the Valley 81
Your Valley Transformed 85
Valley Blessings 95
Valley Decisions 99
Rest in the Valley 101
Your Place of Refuge 105
A Place of Nourishment 109
Letter of Encouragement 113

Photo 2: A mountain and valley in Israel

As you read the bible passages in this book, please take the Logos, *the written words,* off the pages and give them Rhema, *life and power,* in your life. Let the words come alive in you! God did not speak to the writers for the words to merely stay on the pages. The Word of God is meant to bring life through the tongues and into the hearts and lives of the believer. Speak the words into your spirit and be blessed!

The photos in this book, including the cover photo, are from the personal collection of the author. The photo on the cover was taken in Oman in The Middle East.

Photo 3: A herder in Abu Dhabi, UAE

Introduction

- ✝ You are there for everybody else, but no one is there for you.
- ✝ You feel lonely, alone, and rejected.
- ✝ You don't understand this strange place.
- ✝ You were laid off from your job.
- ✝ You've just been told that you have cancer.
- ✝ Your child has just been arrested.
- ✝ You have been molested and abused.
- ✝ You can't sleep at night; secrets have you trapped.
- ✝ The new person on the job, the one that you trained, was promoted to the job you wanted.
- ✝ Nothing you try is working out.
- ✝ You had to walk 10 miles in the snow and rain, because nobody stopped to help.
- ✝ Your best friend has betrayed you.
- ✝ Your spouse has left you.
- ✝ You're in a rut, a mess, in need of deliverance and can't break through.
- ✝ The members of your church shun you.
- ✝ You've been falsely accused; your pastor has betrayed you.
- ✝ You miss your loved one who has passed away.
- ✝ You just need a friend… somebody.

What do you do?

Oh, Saint of God, it is time to *mount up! Arise and shine*! But...

...that's not the way we've been handling situations is it? This is the time to rejoice! But ... that's not our way is it? This is not the time to cry, fuss, complain, get angry, or to have a pity party. No! The power of God needs to be seen through our lives, through all the stuff, through the clouds and darkness. Let the glory of God shine through you!

PART ONE

Tribulation

Valley experiences are often confused with wilderness experiences.

You probably do not want to walk in the wilderness. Although at times, this is necessary. Sometimes you may wander in the wilderness, as the children of Israel did, because of continual disobedience, lack of faith, refusing to turn to God, following men, fleshly lusts and desires. Sometimes you may be called and chosen, like John the Baptist, to preach for a season in the wilderness. You may also have to spend time in the wilderness for the death and burial of your flesh or your character, as you put on the character of Christ.

Unlike the wilderness, however, the valley is for those who are faithfully following Christ, those who are called "His sheep." In this life, you will spend time regularly in the valley. Sometimes in your valley you may "feel" alone, isolated, gloomy and afraid. You may not enjoy the valley at all, but this is exactly the purpose of this book, to dispel common myths and misbeliefs and to let you in on what the valley is really all about.

Wilderness	Valley
Generally wild, uncultivated, desolate, desert place, inhabited only by animals; think of it as the "wild"	*A low place or interval between hills or mountains, usually around a stream; often where a river or glacier once was; refers to a low place in life, a time of fear, doom and gloom*
The Spirit led Jesus to the wilderness to be tempted of the devil. The wilderness is a time and place of temptation.	*Jesus leads His sheep through the valley for peace and nourishment. The valley is a place to be nourished, to be strengthened.*
The Israelites walked in the wilderness 40 years until all the adults, except Joshua and Caleb died, because of their continual disobedience and lack of faith. John preached repentance in the wilderness.	God goes before us to make the crooked places straight and the rough places smooth.
People sometimes went into the wilderness to make sacrifices.	Shepherds lead their sheep into the valley to eat, drink and rest.
When God was angry with His people, He would make their fruitful places like the wilderness—dry and desolate.	Many valleys are full of plush green plants and grass, with flowing water.
Rugged mountains are often in the wilderness.	Mountains are not IN the valley. You get to the next mountain after you've been through the valley. A valley is between mountains.
Sheep get lost in the wilderness.	Sheep are with their shepherd being led through the valley.

God did not choose us for the sole purpose of our own salvation and entrance into His kingdom. Heaven is not our purpose. Heaven is our reward. Our purpose is to be the demonstration and illustration of God's glory, His love and His power. Those who interact with us in any capacity, whether family, friends, co-workers, service representatives, students, employers, employees, enemies or absolute strangers, should be able to see our Father through us. Our love should reflect His love. Our mercy and forgiveness should be a reflection of God's daily renewed mercy and forgiveness. His omnipotence should be revealed through our works and our very lives. Our Father's omniscient wisdom and strength should be demonstrated in us. When people see us, they should see GOD!

For who are we?

> *1Pet 2:9 "But [we] are a chosen generation, a royal priesthood, an holy nation, a peculiar people; that [we] should shew forth the praises of him who hath called [us] out of darkness into his marvelous light:"*

So for this purpose, we must usher victory and power into our lives.

As sheep and followers of God, we are taught how to go through tribulation, but too often, we have held our heads down, too burdened and full of sorrow to give God praise. So many times, we shut ourselves in with spirits of sadness and depression surrounding us. How many days and hours have you spent being angry with yourself and angry with others about situations, and even angry with God? How often have you tried to take matters into your own hands and made a mess of things? Sometimes, we give up on God, blame Him and turn away from the only One who can solve the real problem. The following lessons reveal God's purpose for your valley and the winner's strategy for facing, withstanding, understanding and walking THROUGH each one of your valleys.

First and foremost, please understand that tribulation is a part of life. We all experience tribulation. Whether we suffer as Christians or as sinners, we are going to have tribulation. But as children of God, we face tribulation in a manner unlike the norm for mankind. Let me stress that principle. The children of God view tribulation in a way that is unusual, strange and illogical to the natural way of man.

We *need* to go through the tribulation. There is a reason for every season. There is a method to the madness. If you understand the following lessons, you will forever know and enjoy the joy of the LORD.

LESSON 1

Tribulation is Definite

Strong's dictionary defines tribulation as *"pressure (literal or figurative)—Affliction, anguish, burdens, persecution, trouble."*

> *Job 14:1 "Man that is born of a woman is of few days and full of trouble."*

When we completely understand and accept that trouble is a necessary component of our lives, we may not become so disappointed, so distraught and upset during these tribulations. Even when it seems that you are being buried under one thing after another, there are at least two concepts to consider.

One, that you're being buried with Christ, in order to experience his resurrection power in you. The second is that you're not being buried. Instead, you're being planted. Either way, occasionally, we need to go through the valley in order to reach the mountain. Accepting this truth and learning to praise your way through the valley is the way to get past the trouble, to the next mountain, and to your next level.

Remember, Jesus your Shepherd, is right in front of you, leading and guiding you through it. He's not going to drag you. You must walk. He knows when you are wounded, and you need Him to carry you. He also knows when you're just weak, and it's best for you to rest by the stream to gain strength. Our Shepherd will patiently wait while you gain strength in this valley, but as soon as you put on what you need, you will get through it.

What happened to your joy? Your strength is increased by your joy; and how is joy restored? I remember the old song, "Count your blessings. Name them one by one." Instead of listing your problems, count your blessings! This song goes along with Paul's admonition to the Philippians.

> *Philip 4:8 "Finally, brethren, whatsoever things are true, whatsoever things are honest, whatsoever things are just, whatsoever things are pure, whatsoever things are lovely, whatsoever things are of good report; if there be any virtue, and if there be any praise, think on these things."*

Praise truly is vitally important! Jesus told the people of Nazareth why He came by reading from the book of Isaiah. Isaiah 61:1-3 reads like this:

> *"The Spirit of the Lord GOD [is] upon me; because the LORD hath anointed me to... give unto them the oil of joy for mourning, the garment of praise for the spirit of heaviness; that they might be called trees of righteousness, the planting of the LORD, that he might be glorified."*

We *will* feel pressured. We *will* have afflictions. We *will* have trouble. Tribulations are a part of life. But remember that Jesus told John these words.

> *John 16:33 "These things have I spoken unto you, that in me ye might have peace. In the world ye shall have tribulation: but be of good cheer; I have overcome the world."*

So, what do we do? How do we act? Our bodies are flesh and blood, but we have the Spirit of the powerful God within us! So, we can neither act nor react in like manner as mere man is apt to react. Jesus commanded, *"Be of good cheer"*! That seems hard to do, huh?

"But you just don't understand what I'm going through," you say? Who is God that He doesn't see and know *and* feel? In our flesh, yes, it is hard to be cheerful in some situations, but Job declared, *"Yet in my flesh shall I see God," Job 19:26*. Mount up, Saint of God! Think yourself happy, and get ready to go to the next level!

As Christians, witnesses for Christ, martyrs, not only will we have the common tribulations of mankind, but we will also suffer persecution, and is now the time to have a pity party? Is now the time to become angry or to wonder, "Why me?" Is now the time to look for someone to blame, even yourself? No! Everything that happens to you, Child of God, is ordered or allowed by our loving Father, who knows exactly what is best for us.

> *2Tim 3:12 "Yea, and all that will live godly in Christ Jesus shall suffer persecution."*

Mark 10:30 "But he shall receive an hundredfold now in this time, houses, and brethren, and sisters, and mothers, and children, and lands, with persecutions; and in the world to come eternal life."

Luke 11:49 "Therefore also said the wisdom of God, I will send them prophets and apostles, and some of them they shall slay and persecute:"

Luke 21:12 "But before all these, they shall lay their hands on you, and persecute you, delivering you up to the synagogues, and into prisons, being brought before kings and rulers for my name's sake."

John 15:20 "Remember the word that I said unto you, The servant is not greater than his lord. If they have persecuted me, they will also persecute you;"

When you are persecuted, think of yourself as being like Christ. Praise God for allowing you to be like Him, for creating you in His image, and moving you from glory to glory, through persecutions, with Him.

Expect tribulations and persecutions, and when you are attacked by the enemy, Satan, never think that you are under his command or his power! You are NOT! Satan is ALWAYS under God's command and power, and God has delegated His power and authority to His soldiers and footmen—us!

2Chron 18:18-22 "Again he said, Therefore hear the word of the LORD; I saw the LORD sitting upon his throne, and all the host of heaven standing on his right hand and on his left. And the LORD said, Who shall entice Ahab king of Israel, that he may go up and fall at Ramothgilead? And one spake saying after this manner, and another saying after that manner. Then there came out a spirit, and stood before the LORD, and said, I will entice him. And the LORD said unto him, Wherewith? And he said, I will go out, and be a lying spirit in the mouth of all his prophets. And the LORD said, Thou shalt entice him, and thou shalt also prevail: go out, and do even so. Now therefore, behold, the LORD hath put a lying spirit in the mouth of these thy prophets, and the LORD hath spoken evil against thee."

Satan can only do what God allows or sets in motion for the righteous as well as the unrighteous. God has already established that we will definitely have tribulations. As you travel from pressure to burden to persecution, walk like The Anointed One, with The Anointed One, in The Anointed One, and full of the anointing!

LESSON 2

Tribulations are Necessary

Let's look at the athlete in training. This athlete may be involved in individual or team sports or in special training for the Olympics. This athlete must go through vigorous and rigorous training, often exhausting and painful for the muscles and the entire body. Unless he possesses extraordinary determination and dedication, this person will give up and miss out on the victories of winning.

Those who make it to the championships are all victorious. Even if they do not win a title in the final competitions, they have victory in the fact that "they made it". So it is with the children of God, for *"he that endureth to the end shall be saved." Matthew 10:22*

Pressure in the earth helps to create diamonds. Brushing a horse vigorously results in a beautiful shine. Pressure will cause a bottle to explode, but if the pressure is released just before the bursting point, there will be no explosion. Increased heat and pressure will cause a volcano to eventually erupt. Likewise, the pressure caused by the heat of tribulations will result in an eruption of God's anointing in the believer's life.

You *need* the tribulation. You *need* the pressure. A mother in labor as she is delivering her child, feels the pressure, and therefore feels the urgent need to PUSH! Sometimes you may have to push yourself up to keep moving through your valleys, but accept what God allows. Communicate with the Holy Spirit to know His instructions to you. Obey every single step. He's with you and guiding you through.

> *Acts 14:22 "Confirming the souls of the disciples, and exhorting them to continue in the faith, and that we must through much tribulation enter into the kingdom of God."*
>
> *1Thess 3:4 "For verily, when we were with you, we told you before that we should suffer tribulation;"*

2Cor 4:9 "Persecuted, but not forsaken; cast down, but not destroyed;"

Photo 4: Waterfall from the mountain to the valley below in Alaska

LESSON 3

There is a Reason for the Season

Why is tribulation necessary? Why must we endure such suffering? What reason could there possibly be for this giant that I'm facing? Why must I hurt so badly? The scriptures give us the following answers:

- For your glory
- For your testimony about Christ
- That you may gain patience (for your perfection)
- For the spreading of the gospel
- For the Kingdom—To reign with Christ

Photo 5: The lush vegetation of the Jezreel Valley in Israel

✝
For Your Glory

Ephes 3:13 "Wherefore I desire that ye faint not at my tribulations for you, which is for your glory."

1Pet 1:7 "That the trial of your faith, being much more precious than of gold that perisheth, though it be tried with fire, might be found unto praise and honour and glory at the appearing of Jesus Christ:"

Rom 8:18 "For I reckon that the sufferings of this present time [are] not worthy [to be compared] with the glory which shall be revealed in us."

2Pet 1:3 "According as his divine power hath given unto us all things that [pertain] unto life and godliness, through the knowledge of him that hath called us to glory and virtue:"

The Greek term for glory is "doxa" which means the opinion or judgment that someone is worthy of honor and praise, or a "most glorious condition, most exalted state". This condition or worthiness is gained only after we have endured great tribulation and suffering. God has "called us" to this glory! Since

GOD has "called us" to this glory, all we need to do is follow the call!

Although our final and ultimate glory is hidden until the day Jesus returns, we also experience glory right now, each time Jesus shows up in our situation. So, we can endure this temporary suffering. This will pass. This sickness will pass. This persecution will pass. This season of low income will pass. This present sadness will pass. This time of separation will pass. This dark period in your life will pass. And because you endured with faith and with praise in your heart and on your lips, the glory will come. There will be glory after this!

Isn't it wonderful to know that for all the tribulations we endure, there is glory coming? What are your expectations of glory? What have you asked of God? What is the extent of your faith? Your glory is coming! Praise God! Our tribulations are only leading us to our glory.

Let's look at two body-builders in training, Dave and Joe. They're both working out daily, lifting weights, running, suffering the burning, eating the right foods, and giving up the unhealthy ones. Dave gets tired of the daily dedication, giving up all of his fun time, burgers, chocolate, pizza and drinks with the guys, and he gives up. On the other hand, Joe continues, true to his commitment. He is chided by Dave and the guys now and then, and Dave even tries to persuade Joe to hang out on weekends, but Joe stays the course.

After a while, Joe is looking good, and people are noticing. He can't go anywhere without getting a compliment. The ladies all want to be seen with him. Joe starts entering competitions and winning! His name and picture are on the front pages of sports and fitness magazines. He gets spots in commercials, invitations to schools and other community events, and even invited to appear on talk shows. Joe is getting all the glory now, while Dave continues to be more and more unfit and envious.

Joe would never have experienced the glory if he had given up. If he had not endured the pain and suffering, if he had not stayed focused on his goal in spite of the joking and Dave's attempts to distract him, Joe would not have known the successful feeling of praise and honor.

Endure until the end. Your glory is coming!

Photo 6: A valley in the Yukon of Canada

✞
For Your Testimony about Christ

Rev 1:9 "I, John, who also am your brother, and companion in tribulation, and in the kingdom and patience of Jesus Christ, was in the isle that is called Patmos, for the word of God, and for the testimony of Jesus Christ."

2Tim 3:11 "What persecutions I endured: but out of them all the Lord delivered me."

2Cor 12:10 "Therefore I take pleasure in infirmities, in reproaches, in necessities, in persecutions, in distresses for Christ's sake: for when I am weak, then am I strong."

The disciples, who had been specifically chosen by Christ, were obedient to carry on His works of love and power, preaching and teaching Jesus with signs and wonders following, and setting people free. Their teachings proved man to be sinful and his beliefs erroneous. So, of course, the leaders of the cities persecuted and killed them. Christian persecution didn't just recently begin. It has been going on since the days of Jesus Christ. Instead of killing John, though, they exiled him to be alone on the isle of Patmos until his death, similar to the way some religions exile members of their groups who convert to Christianity today. This exile was John's "punishment" according to man.

Punishment was the *reason* John was on that isle but not the *purpose*. It was the cause but not the end. God had a plan. God always has a plan. The tribulation of his exile sentence actually "led" him to the place God needed him to be to receive the prophetic revelation of future events.

These visions, this revelation that John received from God, were so great and important and so intense that John needed to be totally alone to receive them. God ordered and ordained every step. It was all God. So, John says in Rev 1:9 that he was in the isle *"for the word of God, and for the testimony of Jesus Christ."* How awesome is that?

If you can get excited when tribulation comes, knowing that "this" is your ticket to your next place in God, your ride to glory, then you can make it in the arms of God, your Father. Your tribulation is orchestrated just for you! This is to allow you to be a personal witness and to have your own record, your own report of the power and glory of God. "Make it count!" Be comforted, and relax peacefully and confidently knowing "this" is not coming from man. "This" is not just a situation. No! Man was just the tool God used. He has to use somebody. "This" is an ordained step in your life--ordered directly by your Father. You will be eyewitness to an awesome victory and testify with your own personal report!

Photo 7: Picture taken on a Mt. McKinley tour in Alaska

That You May Gain Patience— And be Complete

Rom 5:3 "And not only so, but we glory in tribulations also: knowing that tribulation worketh patience;"

James 1:3-4 "Knowing this, that the trying of your faith worketh patience. But let patience have her perfect work, that ye may be perfect and entire, wanting nothing."

Heb 10:36 "For ye have need of patience, that, after ye have done the will of God, ye might receive the promise."

1Pet 5:10 "But the God of all grace, who hath called us unto his eternal glory by Christ Jesus, after that ye have suffered a while, make you perfect, stablish, strengthen, settle you."

Rev 2:10 "Fear none of those things which thou shalt suffer: behold, the devil shall cast some of you into prison, that ye may be tried; and ye shall have tribulation ten days: be thou faithful unto death, and I will give thee a crown of life."

Impatient people may become angry and frustrated easily. They may become irritable. They may get depressed. And who enjoys being around that type of character?

When you lose patience, you may sling words that you wish you could take back, and you can't. That's when you may behave in ways that you regret later.

What exactly is patience? The Greek equivalent is *"hypomone,"* being steadfast and unmovable in one's faith and reverence for God, a deliberate decision to not be swayed by even the most unbelievable trials and sufferings. Patience is such a strong concept that James refers to it as a separate character from one's own. James admonishes us to allow patience to have "her" perfect work.

If we are to "let" patience, then we must already have the capacity to be patient. If we are to "let" patience, then our own actions, plans, strategies and thoughts must fight against the very character that needs to dominate. When we stop fighting, stop trying to be in control, be still and "let" patience work, then we will see God's finished product. When God gets finished, nothing else will be needed, for we will be complete, full grown, and mature. We will not want *("leipo"—leave behind, forsake, be destitute of, lag behind or be inferior to)* anything! Your victory, success, attitude, atmosphere, and witness to the world all depend on your surrender to patience.

If you quickly recognize the reasons for your tribulations, you are more apt to be steadfast, patiently waiting with praise until you reach your breakthrough. You will be able to proclaim as Job proclaimed in Job 14:14, *"All the days of my appointed time will I wait, till my change come."* You will have and hold in your heart this determination, *"Though he slay me, yet will I trust in Him,"* Job 13:15.

"Time" in that verse does not indicate hours, months, or years. What it does indicate in its Hebrew origin is "hard service" as in doing time or serving a sentence doing hard time in prison. Did you get that? Every day of this hard service, I'm just going to be patient and wait, because I know my change is coming. I know my Redeemer still lives. I am on my way to a new level of glory. Thank You, Jesus!

Knowing why we have tribulation can excite or relax us and help us to be patient during each time of suffering or trouble. As you become more and more patient, your attitude, personality and demeanor will be perfected, and you will be more complete within yourself and as a soldier in God's Kingdom.

For the Spreading of the Gospel

Matt 10:23 "But when they persecute you in this city, flee ye into another: for verily I say unto you, Ye shall not have gone over the cities of Israel, till the Son of man be come."

Acts 11:19 "Now they which were scattered abroad upon the persecution that arose about Stephen travelled as far as Phenice, and Cyprus, and Antioch, preaching the word."

When men wanted to build a tower to reach "unto heaven," or the visible sky, they had the intelligence and the ability to do just that. God created man to be highly intelligent. God prevented that Tower of Babel from being finished by causing them all to speak a different language, thus babbling to each other.

Since they could not understand each other, they had to stop building. These people separated from one another, scattered, and began to populate the whole world instead of just one area. This wonderful, colorful, and interesting world of diverse people and cultures actually began because of trouble. They could no longer understand each other.

Leaving a place because of persecution is not necessarily because of that place you're coming from. What is more important is that place you are on your way to. Where are you going, and what are you going to do when you get there? What does God need you to do in this next destination? Abraham had to leave his kin, his familiar ground to go to the Promised Land. What is your promised land? Where are you going? Where is this tribulation taking you? Where are these persecutions taking you?

Analyze your tribulations, your troubles, your afflictions. For which of these reasons might you be going through right now? For glory? For a testimony? Because you have need of patience? Because God wants to prepare you for your crown? Is it time to move on to another place in God, with God, or for God? There *is* a reason for the season! "God, my Father, what is it that you are doing in me?"

For the Kingdom—To Reign With Christ

Finally, and most importantly, Jesus instructs us in Matthew 6:33 that our priority must be to seek the kingdom of God and his righteousness.

> *"But seek ye first the kingdom of God, and his righteousness; and all these things shall be added unto you."*

The word "kingdom" is translated from the Greek word *"basileia"* and means "royal power, kingship, dominion, rule; the right or authority to rule." So, more than anything, we are to seek for the kingship, the authority or the right to rule with God.

Paul clarifies the kingdom of God even more for us.

> *Rom 14:17 "For the kingdom of God is not meat and drink; but righteousness, and peace, and joy in the Holy Ghost."*

The kingdom of God is righteousness. Righteousness is the condition of being acceptable to God, being correct in your actions, feelings and even your thoughts, integrity, purity. How do we obtain righteousness and this authority to rule with God? Exactly how do we obtain this supreme kingship?

Paul explains that we obtain the kingdom through suffering for Christ. There is a saying in society that we don't know someone until we have walked a mile in their shoes. It is believed that we don't truly know someone until we have suffered through perilous times with them. This is founded on one of the utmost spiritual principles that is preached and taught by several of God's writers.

> *2Tim 2:12 "If we suffer, we shall also reign with him:"*
>
> *Colos 1:24, NLT "I am glad when I suffer for you in my body, for I am participating in the sufferings of Christ that continue for his body, the church."*
>
> *Philip 3:10 "That I may know him, and the power of his resurrection, and the fellowship of his sufferings, being made conformable unto his death;"*
>
> *2Corin 11:23-33 "... If I must needs glory, I will glory of the things which concern mine infirmities..."*
>
> *2Corin 12:9-13 "... Therefore I take pleasure in infirmities, in reproaches, in necessities, in persecutions, in distresses for Christ's sake: for when I am weak, then am I strong."*

> *Philip 1:14, NLT "And because of my imprisonment, most of the believers here have gained confidence and boldly speak God's message without fear."*
>
> *Philip 1:29, NLT "For you have been given not only the privilege of trusting in Christ but also the privilege of suffering for him."*
>
> *Heb 11:25 "Choosing rather to suffer affliction with the people of God, than to enjoy the pleasures of sin for a season;"*

Jesus, Himself, gave similar instructions concerning the importance of suffering and what to do when we suffer.

> *Matt 5:11-12 "Blessed are ye, when men shall revile you, and persecute you, and shall say all manner of evil against you falsely, for my sake. Rejoice, and be exceeding glad: for great is your reward in heaven: for so persecuted they the prophets which were before you."*
>
> *Luke 6:22-23 "Blessed are ye, when men shall hate you, and when they shall separate you from their company, and shall reproach you, and cast out your name as evil, for the Son of man's sake. Rejoice ye in that day, and leap for joy: for, behold, your reward is great in heaven:"*

> *Luke 14:27 "And whosoever doth not bear his cross, and come after me, cannot be my disciple."*

Peter also rejoiced in his suffering and continued the teachings of Jesus.

> *1Pet 1:7 Jubilee Bible 2000 "that the trial of your faith, being much more precious than of gold (which perishes, nevertheless it is tried with fire), might be found unto praise and glory and honour when Jesus, the Christ, is made manifest"*

> *1Pet 4:12-16 "Beloved, think it not strange concerning the fiery trial which is to try you, as though some strange thing happened unto you: But rejoice, inasmuch as ye are partakers of Christ's sufferings; that, when his glory shall be revealed, ye may be glad also with exceeding joy... if any man suffer as a Christian, let him not be ashamed; but let him glorify God on this behalf."*

So, with the witnesses of all these scriptures, Jesus tell us to seek the kingdom of God, the kingship, the ruling authority of God instead of seeking even our basic needs. Our priority is to seek the kingdom and God's righteousness. We are to seek to suffer, not to avoid suffering. We are to seek for the opportunity to stand up and to speak for Christ, not run from these situations. We are to look for opportunities to testify, to be a witness for Jesus Christ every day and any time.

We suffer so that we may rule with God. We suffer that we may inherit the kingdom, the kingship of God, the right and authority to rule with God.

The time of suffering is not the time to be depressed or to give up. The time of suffering is the time to rejoice exceedingly!

LESSON 4

Let Go of Your Old Way

Think about how you have handled your troubles or not handled them in the past. How do you normally act or react to adverse circumstances? What do you do when things aren't going the way you want them to go? What do you do when it seems like Satan is having a field day in your life? Take a moment to think about that. Do you remember that Satan is only *as* a roaring lion, but Jesus Christ the Lamb of God *is* the "Lion of the tribe of Judah"? So, what should you do in the face of tribulation, in the eye of the tornado?

We must get rid of our old ways.

> *Rom 8:35 "Who shall separate us from the love of Christ? Shall tribulation, or distress, or persecution, or famine, or nakedness, or peril, or sword?"*

There are times when we do allow all of these things to carry us into a place of doubting God or wondering where He is or when He's coming to deliver us, to heal us, to make everything all right. Truthfully and realistically, we are sometimes moved from a place of joyful praise and worship to a gloomy, painful, weakened existence and attitude. Why? Often, we will not feel the love of God when we are going through our tribulations, because our focus is not on God but on the situation and ourselves. We forget about the "love" of God at the time, and separate ourselves from this love.

We separate ourselves from this love by the way we treat those who seem to be causing our trouble. We fail to see these tribulations as part of God loving us. We start to think that He's turned His back on us, or that we're being punished.

Let us remember that whatever comes our way, God is in control! Trust God! That's all. Trust God! When you know that you are in the will of God, and you have been obeying Him, just trust Him. God knows that you love Him. This is for you! This, too, will pass! And in what condition will you be after the storm? Will you have gone to the next level or will you have gone backwards a couple of steps? Will you be like a tree planted and still standing?

> *Mark 4:17 "And have no root in themselves, and so endure but for a time: afterward, when affliction or persecution ariseth for the word's sake, immediately they are offended."*

This scripture explains that sometimes affliction and persecution happens for the sake of the Word. Either to demonstrate what the Word of God says so that people will believe, or because the Word of God, as the double-edged sword it is cuts to the truth, and some people don't want the truth to be known.

This reminds me of something my husband always says when I get angry or appalled with something that happens on TV. Sometimes, I'll scream at the TV, "Why did you do that?!" He never gets ruffled. He's always so calm, and he'll just say, "Because it's in the script." He has said this so often, that now, we say it together, right after I've screamed at the TV again. The plan of God is written in His Word. If it is "in the script" the truth of God's Word will be seen, no doubt about it. Let's put off the old way, pay attention to God, and recognize His hand in every aspect of our lives.

Do you find yourself easily upset or offended? We must get rid of the old ways of responding to tribulation—anger, worry, depression, head down, confusion, can't open your mouth to give God praise, complaining, stubbornness, etc. We must put off the old and put on the new. Because, my friend, all of this is for you!

LESSON 5

God's Way for Us

"There is a way that seemeth right unto a man but the end thereof [are] the ways of death." Prov 14:12

After putting off the way you used to view tribulation, let us look at what God's Word reveals to us about how we *should* deal with tribulation and persecution. I've divided the ways into three categories:

- ✝ *Be Joyful*
- ✝ *Be Patient*
- ✝ *Bless and Be a Comfort To Others*

Photo 8: A fertile valley in Israel

☦
Be Joyful

Joyful in tribulations? How in the world are we supposed to be joyful in the midst of pressure? These burdens are so heavy! How am I supposed to be joyful? Am I supposed to rejoice when I am being persecuted? Really? I was just asked to leave my church. Hallelujah! The whole neighborhood just beat my husband to a bloody pulp and burned down my house! Oh, thank You, Jesus! Really?

How can I rejoice when all I feel like doing is crying? Isn't it all right to cry? The Bible says that, *"Weeping may endure for a night..."Psalm 30:5* How am I supposed to rejoice when I am weeping through the night? When my family seems to face trouble after trouble, what do I rejoice about? When our house has burned down, and we have lost everything, how do I rejoice? When my spouse has just told me, "I don't love you anymore," how am I supposed to rejoice after *that?*

Are any of these questions your thoughts? Your feelings? Sometimes, I've wanted to just lie in my bed, with no one to bother me, and get a good cry in.

I've not only felt like doing that, but I have done just that. Let me tell you about the time when I learned to praise God with victory through my tears of sorrow.

It was during a time when I felt like everything in my life was crumbling all around me. I even questioned my relationship with God, to the point when the enemy slipped a question in my mind concerning the reality of *God! (From my childhood, through my own personal experiences, I have always known that God is real—without a doubt!)* My heart was broken, and I felt like my life was backwards and messed up, and nothing I was trying to do was working for me or anyone else anymore. I felt betrayed, rejected, hopeless, helpless, abandoned, isolated and alone.

I was on my knees praying, talking to God about my sorrows and crying my heavy, heavy broken heart out to Him. He reminded me that He gives us, not just "*a*" garment but "*the* garment of praise for the spirit of heaviness."

But there was no praise in me. I didn't *feel like* praising anybody! I wanted my heart healed, and my spirit lifted out of that heaviness, though, so while I was in the midst of crying and feeling so heavy, I just began to offer up praise, because Jesus is always worthy. I began to thank Him just for being God. I began to thank Him for what I was going through and whatever He was doing through it or going to do through it and because of it. I began to thank Him for His love for me.

I just praised God, because I knew that was the way out—not because I felt like praising Him. I praised God, because I did *not* feel like it, because I knew that Satan did not want me to praise Him. I praised God, because I knew that if I didn't, I might stay in that situation for a long time. Mostly, I just praised Him in obedience to His Word—just because the Bible says to.

That was my first experience of praising God through tears of real sorrow, and you know what? I really did feel much better afterwards! I felt stronger and victorious! The more I praised, the more I wanted to praise, and the more victorious the praise became! The more I praised God, the more He lifted me!

I started with just saying and reciting the regular old words of praise, while on my knees crying. Then, the words became heartfelt cries, then shouts of praise. Then, it sounded as if my praise became warfare praise, and I was up on my feet. Then, I was jumping around the room. The next thing I knew, I was running from the bed to the door, then down the hall and all over my home!

By the time I stopped for a break, I was delivered! I had come through! And, I had some answers to my situations, too!

That happened many years ago, but even more recently, a little more than one month ago, I was in sorrow over the death of someone extremely dear to me. This sorrow had me almost emotionally paralyzed, if you can imagine the meaning of that. I was on the floor, late in the night, thinking and listening for God, needing to get myself together. I knew she was in a better place, and I knew she was happy. As I sat there on that floor giving God thanks, there was peace but no real joy or happiness. As I continued to thank God for different details concerning her, God spoke to me again through the words of a song, and before the end of the song, tears of joy were streaming down my face, and I was shouting wonderful praise to God from an uplifted heart.

I could have chosen to remain in that state of sorrow and gloom, but the praises of God brought me out of that condition, so that I could finally be joyous during the time of sorrow, and I could function again. Oh, yes. There are still times when I feel sadness, but I don't allow the sadness to linger long enough to have a party and invite gloom and depression. I remember the joy. And I smile.

Let's look at some scriptures.

> *Rev 7:14 "These are they which came out of great tribulation, and have washed their robes, and made them white in the blood of the Lamb."*
>
> *2Cor 8:2 "How that in a great trial of affliction the abundance of their joy and their deep poverty abounded unto the riches of their liberality."*
>
> *Rom 5:3 "And not only so, but we glory in tribulations also: knowing that tribulation worketh patience;"*
>
> *2Cor 12:10 "Therefore I take pleasure in infirmities, in reproaches, in necessities, in persecutions, in distresses for Christ's sake: for when I am weak, then am I strong."*
>
> *2Cor 7:4 "I am filled with comfort, I am exceeding joyful in all our tribulation."*
>
> *Matt 5:10-12 "Blessed are they which are persecuted for righteousness' sake: for theirs is the kingdom of*

heaven. Blessed are ye, when men shall revile you, and persecute you, and shall say all manner of evil against you falsely, for my sake. Rejoice, and be exceeding glad: for great is your reward in heaven: for so persecuted they the prophets which were before you."

Out of the mouths of two or three witnesses let every word be established. Thus, we've heard from Brothers John, Paul and Matthew in the above scriptures. Aren't these more than enough witnesses to stress to us that we *must* rejoice in the midst of persecutions, trials and tribulations? Rejoice!

This is our time to ruffle Satan. To tell him he does not have nor is he getting the victory. No matter what it looks like, feels like, seems like, smells like, or tastes like, he does not have the victory in your life, not in your home, not in your situations, not over your emotions, Not! Not! Not! Then, rejoice until Satan is dumbfounded, confused, messed up and has to flee for another season!

To take pleasure in infirmities, in persecutions, in distresses…this seems a hard thing to do sometimes. It even seems impossible! But now is the time for true victory! Is your current battle your hottest ever? Ahhh… This is a great victory about to happen!

In the NCAA and the ACC basketball tournaments, the best games and the best victories are those won after a tough battle, after the game has gone into overtime because of ties. Likewise, the sweeter victory is always after the toughest battles.

Paul, Matthew, and John, among others, are witnesses of what rejoicing *in* tribulation will do for us! Have you ever tried it? How did you feel while you were rejoicing? How did you feel after rejoicing?

Paul said that it was *in* affliction and tribulation when he had "abundance" of joy. He stated that he was "filled" with comfort and "exceeding" joyful! Paul further declared that he takes "pleasure" in his persecutions! *Takes pleasure in his persecutions!* Whew! What a testimony!

Jesus, Himself, tells us in the gospel according to St. Matthew, to be "exceeding" glad! And in a previous scripture, Peter tells us to go on and rejoice now, because we'll be glad later with "exceeding" joy! So, if you've never tried rejoicing during your tribulation and persecutions, just do it! Rejoice your way through!

Photo 9: A close-up view of a small section of the Jezreel Valley in Israel

✠
Be Patient

As long as we continue to rejoice and to give God praise in our suffering, we will gain strength. With this strength, we can be patient to endure, to suffer long, until our change comes.

> *Psalm 30:5 "Weeping may endure for a night but joy cometh in the morning."*
>
> *Gen 1:5 "And the evening and the morning were the first day."*

Please understand that the day doesn't *end* with the evening. Biblically, the day *begins* with the evening. If the "ninth hour" of the day is 3:00PM, then the first hour of the Hebrew day starts at 7:00 AM, and the 12th hour of the day is at 6:00PM. With this calendar, the day ends at 6:59 in the morning. The day ends with the morning—the joy! At the end, there is joy! When it's all over, *joy*! We get to rejoice over that trouble twice—once while we're in it, then we get to rejoice again because of the victory, after we've come through! Hallelujah!

Let's look at more scriptures.

1 Cor 4:12 tells us that *"being persecuted, we suffer it."* The word *suffer* in this verse is the Greek word *anechomai* meaning "to hold oneself up against". Did you get that? To hold oneself *up*—not leaning, not lying down, not keeled over from the pressure, *up*-- and not up with the crowd or with the majority, but up *against*.

> *Ephes 6:13 "Wherefore take unto you the whole armour of God, that ye may be able to withstand in the evil day, and having done all, to stand."*

There's no need for you to fight this battle. You simply fight the fight of faith. *Hold* to your faith! You need the whole armour so that you can "stand against" the enemy. That's it! Just stand against the deceptions of the enemy. Nothing he shows you is truth or real. They are all deceptions! Hold to your faith! Be patient, and resist the enemy. Persevere! Endure! Stand! God will fight all your battles. You just fight the battle between yourself and the enemy of your mind, as he tries to take away your faith. It was Abraham's faith that was tested, and it was this same faith that was counted unto him for righteousness. Don't let the devil fool you, deceive you, influence you, or trap you. Keep the faith, and *stand*!

> *Rom 12:12 "patient in tribulation; continuing instant in prayer ..."*
>
> *Job 14:14 "... all the days of my appointed time will I wait, 'til my change come."*

The Hebrew word for *time* in this scripture is *tsaba* meaning, "hardship" or "hard service". This term was discussed earlier, but I want to make an interesting note that in Strong's concordance, right beside the word *hardship* is the word *worship*! *Hardship* and *worship* are synonymous in this case! So then, could we also read that verse as, "*...all the days of my appointed worship...*"? So, this hard service, this hardship I'm going through is appointed to me for my worship time as well? So, do you mean this is *my* time to spend privately and personally with my Savior? Look where the comma (and therefore a pause) is! "*...will I wait*"... "*...til my change come.*" Hallelujah! Your change is coming!

Photo 10: Another view of the Jezreel Valley

Bless and be a Comfort to Others

Share what God has given to you when you've made it through the storm or while you are still making it through, but you are stronger now. Bless others. Comfort somebody else and help them to go through their storm. Yes, even when they may have hurt you or were not there for you. Even when they have nothing good at all to say to you, *bless them.*

God will continue comforting you even as you are comforting others. God will continue to bless you as you are blessing others. And the whole body will be encouraged, fitly joined together as one, lifting up the name of Jesus together. Talk about the demons being confused! They will *have* to flee! What a time! What a time! What a time!

> *2Cor 1:4 "Who comforteth us in all our tribulation, that we may be able to comfort them which are in any trouble, by the comfort wherewith we ourselves are comforted of God."*

> *Rom 12:14 "Bless them which persecute you: bless, and curse not."*

> *1Cor 4:12 "being reviled, we bless"*
>
> *Matt 5:44 "But I say unto you, Love your enemies, bless them that curse you, do good to them that hate you, and pray for them which despitefully use you, and persecute you."*
>
> *Luke 22:32 "And the Lord said,... behold, Satan hath desired to have you, that he may sift you as wheat: But I have prayed for thee, that they faith fail not: and when thou art converted, strengthen thy brethren."*

God comforts us so that we will be able to comfort our sisters and brothers, our loved ones, our children, even strangers. We comfort through our fellowship, our actions, our admonition, our prayers, our testimonies, our positive atmosphere, our smiles, our love, our ability to share a word from our Father, our lives and our giving of ourselves.

Isn't that how the Holy Spirit comforts us? Through His fellowship with us, His ways and actions, His positive, caring, and loving presence, His Word, through God pouring Himself into and onto us? So, likewise, we must do the same for others. This is how the body is fitly joined together as one.

When we do what Jesus instructed and *commanded* us to do in Matthew 5:44, love, "do good to", and pray for our enemies, we will have peace. When we keep our minds focused on God and not on ourselves, we will have *perfect* peace.

Seriously? Love our enemies? Those who make it hard for anyone to love them? Those who deserve punishment rather than blessings (like Jonah and the city of Nineveh)? Yes! Those, the ones you wish could be taken off the face of the earth, because they cause so much turmoil and heartache. Yes! Love them! Jesus *commanded* us to love them and to "do good to" them. And remember that "love" is demonstrated more through actions than with words. *Pray for them!*

There is great joy when they repent unto salvation, when they come to the realization of how evil they have been, fall to their knees crying out to God for mercy, turn from their wicked ways to serve a loving God, then come again to you, apologizing and testifying of the great change that has taken place in their lives! What a great miracle of transformation!

Photo 11: A valley in the Denali Mountains, Alaska

Part Two

The Valley

What is a valley? The valley is the low land surrounded by higher land, such as hills and mountains. There is usually a stream or river running through a valley, and sometimes the valley is carved out by a larger river that once existed and is drying or has dried out. Often, you will find lush vegetation in a valley, since the ground has been wet, rich with minerals and quite fertile.

Because it is low land, the analogy of a valley refers to a sad, depressed or low point in one's life. This is interesting, however, because a valley is often filled with more living, growing vegetation than can be seen elsewhere. If one is lost and walking through a desert, it will be his great fortune to come upon a valley where he can find water, shade and possibly something to eat.

Yes, the valley is a low place, but what is the purpose for the valley? If I am *"in the valley"* in my life, what does that really mean for me? Let us go for a walk, a short tour—through the valley.

LESSON 6

God of the Valley

1Kings 20:28 "And there came a man of God, and spake unto the king of Israel, and said, Thus saith the Lord, Because the Syrians have said, The Lord is God of the hills, but he is not God of the valleys, therefore will I deliver all this great multitude into thine hand, and ye shall know that I am the Lord."

Isaiah 40:3-5 "Every valley shall be exalted, and every mountain and hill shall be made low: and the crooked shall be made straight, and the rough places plain: And the glory of the Lord shall be revealed, and all flesh shall see it together: for the mouth of the Lord hath spoken it."

Photo 12: A small waterfall in a valley (wadi) in the country of Oman

A valley is a low area in the surface of the earth that occurs between ranges of mountains, hills or other uplands. Because of this low geographical position, the term "valley" often refers to the condition of loneliness, sadness, trouble, burdens, and danger, anytime when one's emotions are low or down for a period of time.

Have you ever wondered that right after God has awesomely blessed you, right after a shut-in or a few days of prayer and fasting, right after you've had a great day, right after you've been feeling wonderful, as if on a mountain high … you're faced with a great trial or temptation? The valley is between your mountains.

Throughout the Old Testament, armies met in valleys to fight. Wars, battles, and other struggles were very common in valleys, thus they were also places of many victories. Do you feel like you are in a valley? Don't worry. You're just on your way to the next mountain in your life.

> *Deut 8:7 "For the Lord thy God bringeth thee into a good land, a land of brooks of water, of fountains and depths that spring out of valleys and hills."*

The mountain behind you was just a hill compared to the mountain that is ahead. Look forward to what is in store just for you. Look beyond the valley.

> *Heb 12:2 "Looking unto Jesus the author and finisher of our faith; who for the joy that was set before him endured the cross, despising the shame, and is set down at the right hand of the throne of God."*

When the water around you gets so rough and appears to be life-threatening, don't be like Peter, looking and concentrating on the wind and waves. No!

> *Psalm 121:2 "Lift up [your] eyes unto the hills from whence cometh [your] help. [Your] help cometh from the Lord."*

Peter had to look up and reach out to Jesus! Look *up* at the mountain that is yet in front of you. Look *up* at the height you are about to reach in your life!

> *2Corin 5:7 "Walk by faith not by sight."*

> *2Corin 4:17-18 "For our light affliction, which is but for a moment, worketh for us a far more exceeding and eternal weight of glory; while we look not at the things which are seen, but at the things which are not seen:*

> *for the things which are seen are temporal; but the things which are not seen are eternal."*

The topic of the valley is quite deep, but in this mini-lesson, we will only touch the surface, giving a few scriptures. Hopefully, you will partake in a personal Bible Study to delve more deeply into this topic, to more thoroughly understand why the Shepherd leads His sheep through the valley. Psalm 23 is loaded!

When we focus on just the fourth verse of Psalm 23, we are greatly encouraged. Let's look at it. Yes, we will simply touch this psalm by giving reference to only one verse.

> *"Yea, though I walk through the valley in the shadow of death I will fear no evil; for thou art with me; thy rod and thy staff; they comfort me."*

Walking, rather than crawling, denotes strength, maturity and courage. Equally important, walking, instead of running, denotes a slower pace. There is no need to rush through the valley. For we walk by faith, with the strength of God and with courage. We are not running this life by faith, not running away, not trying to get away from anything. We walk by faith, because we are confident, relaxed and are sure that God is leading us to our wealthy place and enlarging our territory.

When we run, we often miss what we would see, hear and otherwise experience if we were only walking. Why did David "walk" through this valley? He knew with certainty that the Shepherd was "with" him. He loved the presence of God, walking with Him, and experiencing life with Him. David often wrote and sang of longing for God, longing to be close to the Shepherd and Lover of his soul.

> *Psalm 42:1 "As the hart panteth after the water brooks, so panteth my soul after thee, O God."*

David perhaps determined, "Father, if it is in the valley that you walk with me, then, let me go through my valley! I won't miss anything that you're leading me to." Let me walk *through* it, not simply *in* it, but through it, for "through" connotes completion, fulfillment. When Jesus had a mission to fulfill in Samaria, He couldn't just walk around it or past it. John 4:4 says, *"...he must needs go through Samaria."* It was necessary for Jesus to go *through* the city.

Refuse to go around this valley! Refuse to turn around and go back to where you were. You've come this far, and you can keep on moving. Go through the valley. There's something here for you, or your Shepherd, your Jehovah-Jireh, your Provider, your *"Everything,"* would not have *led* you here. Jesus leads us into and through the valley.

Let's look at the word *shadow*. Why not just the *valley of death?* The "valley of death" alone would indicate that the Good Shepherd leads His own sheep to definite death.

First of all, Jesus, Himself, is *the Life.* Death and life cannot be in the same body. As soon as *life* comes, there is no more death.

As Satan is *like* a roaring lion, but *not* a lion, so the valley has only the "shadow" of death, but it is *not* death. In the very place where the Shepherd leads you for your nourishment and growth, in the very place that represents life, the enemy, which is death, cannot go, so he has to send a reflection of himself.

He sends something you can see to distract your vision. A shadow does not make a sound. A shadow cannot touch you. A shadow is not the real thing! A shadow can be in front of you, behind you, or beside you, but can never be exactly in the same place as you. A shadow can never hurt you! However, if your focus is on the shadow, you will not walk straight. You will not see what is real. You can hurt *yourself.* You will not see what is true. You will miss what God wants to show you. You will miss your growth, because of ... a *shadow*.

If the sun is behind you, your shadow is cast in front of you. However, if the sun is in front of you, your shadow is cast behind you. If you allow the Son, Jesus Christ, Our Shepherd, to walk in front of you and lead you, the shadow of death will not be before you. Your focus will not be on the shadow, but on the Son. You neither see nor pay attention to the shadow of death, because it is behind you. You don't see it.

As long as you keep the Son before you... as long as you allow the Son to be your Shepherd and lead you—the "shadow" will never overtake you, will never get in front of you to become your focus. Because of that shadow behind you, surely, goodness and mercy shall follow you all the days of your life. Because the shadow is back there, goodness and mercy always follow you, forever there between you and the shadow, protecting your vision, shielding your focus, and comforting you.

That leads us to *"thy rod and thy staff they comfort me..."*

The rod represents miracles, provision, and "the way". According to Exodus 4:5, God anointed the rod that was in Moses's hand for this reason.

> *"That they may believe that the Lord God of their fathers, the God of Abraham, the God of Isaac, and the God of Jacob, hath appeared unto thee."*

Using this rod, Moses performed miracles for the children of Israel. Using this rod, a way was made through the waters, and the children of Israel walked on dry ground to escape the Egyptian army.

No matter how discouraging and difficult the journey became, no matter how tough and hindering the obstacles were, with the rod, God showed His children over and over again that He was present with them, as they walked through their wilderness.

When God shows up to show out in our circumstances, we are comforted; we are encouraged; we are excited and more than excited! We are elated by His grand and divine appearance! Why? Because we know, "It is *on* now!"

With the staff, one leads and guides. The staff helps in various ways on a journey, especially going through rough terrain or rough land with a lot of rocks.

Sometimes the staff is also used for carrying a large supply of food. You may have seen old caricatures or other illustrations depicting men on a journey and carrying a long staff with a handkerchief or bag of food on the upper end. When we allow Christ Jesus to lead our way, He will provide all of our needs. When we are traveling through the rough times of our life, we are comforted, set at ease, released from our pains, our sorrows, and our burdens, because we know and follow our Shepherd.

The crooked places our Shepherd will make straight, and the high places, He will bring down. We don't even have to pray for the straightening of the crooked place. Papa will show up and change the place itself! God's presence will change the very atmosphere! Our Shepherd, with His staff, will remove the damaging rocks that are supposed to hurt us or to cause us to stumble or fall, twist our ankle, or break our toe. He is our bridge over the deep holes or crevices in the ground. We can walk on deep water, or if you're not ready for that yet, He will lift you and carry you through it. He will take us through any obstacle that would zap us of our strength, stamina and energy. When our human energy is gone, our Shepherd carries us.

The shepherd's staff often allows him to rest along the journey. Picture a shepherd resting, leaning on or against his staff. This type of rest is not a complete, unconscious rest, but a relaxed rest, while remaining alert, ready, not lying down and drifting into oblivion there in the valley, but a short, temporary rest, with the indication of soon moving on, focused, and moving on.

Photo 13: Sheep being led by a Bedouin Shepherd in Israel

LESSON 7

The Valley of Vision

Isaiah 22:1-7, NET "Here is a message about the Valley of Vision: What is the reason that all of you go up to the rooftops? The noisy city is full of raucous sounds; the town is filled with revelry. Your slain were not cut down by the sword; they did not die in battle. All your leaders ran away together – they fled to a distant place; all your refugees were captured together – they were captured without a single arrow being shot. So I say, 'Don't look at me! I am weeping bitterly. Don't try to console me concerning the destruction of my defenseless people.'... Your very best valleys were full of chariots; horsemen confidently took their positions at the gate."

When you are burdened because you *see* or sense trouble coming, just know that Jehovah Sabaoth, *the Lord of hosts*, has tens of thousands of angels ready to send out to your valley in your time of trouble. Jehovah Shammah, *the Lord is there*, is already with you, for He is with you all the time. Go on and praise and worship in your Father's presence for your goods are on the way.

God allows you to discern the coming trouble to prepare you. He helps you always to be ready for whatever is to come. You are equipped with the strength that you need for the storm ahead.

Sometimes, while we are in the midst of the storm, we look around us, at the human impossibility of our standing this storm. Like Peter, we begin to sink into those hurts, that trouble, those disappointments, those times of not understanding. We sink into our humanness, rather than our godliness, our spirit form. We lose face of the fact that we are created in God's very image.

Let us not forget that God has prepared us for this, and that *yes*! This *too* will pass! Abba, our Father, our Papa walks us through the valley of vision, so that we can "see". Break forth in praise, for you are now in a place where you can see the whole story! Erupt in volcanic praise for now you can see the *"little cloud out of the sea, like a man's hand." 1 Kings 18:44* You can hear the sound of an abundance of rain. Your help is on the way! You can see your long-awaited blessing finally coming through!

Photo 14: A wadi in the country of Oman

LESSON 8

God's Anger in the Valley

Isaiah 28:17-22 "Judgment also will I lay to the line, and righteousness to the plummet, and the hail shall sweep away the refuge of lies, and the waters shall overflow the hiding place. And your covenant with death shall be disannulled, and your agreement with hell shall not stand; ... From the time that it goeth forth it shall take you: ... For the bed is shorter than that a man can stretch himself on it: and the covering narrower than that he can wrap himself in it. For the Lord shall rise up as in Mount Perazim, he shall be wroth as in the valley of Gibeon, that he may do his work, his strange work; and bring to pass his act, his strange act...for I have heard from the Lord God of hosts a consumption, even determined upon the whole earth."

God measures everyone's righteousness by the plumb line or the plummet, not by each other's acts or another's "righteousness" or what someone else did. God measures what we do by what He, Himself, commanded—bottom line. No one will be able to hide behind any excuse. God is angry with His people for all the sin being committed. Some have made an "agreement with hell" wherein they have the form of godliness, but deny the power, by still holding on to sin and fleshly desires.

Fleshly lusts always war against the soul. From the beginning of the earth, fornication has been the downfall of mankind. God's instructions warn us to flee fornication, but it seems we run towards it at high speed, and it's getting worse. Don't make the mistake of believing that fleshly lusts only deal with sex though. No! A fleshly lust is any carnal desire that satisfies the flesh and has nothing to do with bringing glory to God.

A desire to do what will feed your ego or bring you personal pride or make "you look good" is a fleshly lust. The desire for a position just to boost yourself as a man or woman or just to satisfy a lifetime goal is a fleshly lust. These often go against the will of God for your life. The attention should never be on self. The attention should always be reflected back to God, our Maker, to give glory to God.

We don't want to fall into the hands of an angry God, so while we're in our valley, we must leave all sin there, so that our flight up the next mountain will be possible. We must put off the sin and the weights that so quickly attack, surround and hinder us, so we won't have to stay in the valley so long. Just as in outer space where everything becomes weightless and floats without man's control, we need to be "weightless" so that higher heights are possible for us, and we can move beyond the limits of what is familiar and what we're used to.

Yes! We must move on up to the outer limits, the higher dimensions where there is NO LIMIT! We cannot soar if we remain in the valley. We cannot work for God and bring Him glory in the valley. We must mount up! We must launch out into the deep. We must use the tools that our Father has given to us and work! Go! Move! Show the world our Savior!

Photo 15: Trees, plants and beautiful water of a valley in Oman

LESSON 9

Your Valley Transformed

Jeremiah 31:40 "And the whole valley of the dead bodies, and of the ashes, and all the fields unto the brook of Kidron, unto the corner of the horse gate toward the east, shall be holy unto the Lord; it shall not be plucked up, nor thrown down any more forever."

When we get to the realm of holiness where our spirits are more in control than our bodies— Oh, My God! What a realm of holiness that will be! For our spirits are willing, but that old flesh is weak! When bodily pleasure is "dead", when "my way" is dead, when "that's just me" is dead, when what "I think" is dead, *then* that place, that temple, that vessel, will indeed be "holy unto the Lord". No, not after the spirit is separated from the body—but when sin no longer has control of the body or the mind.

While we yet remain in our earthly bodies, we must be examples of holiness, to let the devil know that God's creation *can* and *will* be holy! Lucifer did not succeed in remaining holy, but we can prove, by the mercies and power of God, that the creation God made a little lower than the angels is able to love God enough to be holy unto Him. Is that your goal? Is that your desire? Is that your longing?

Let us not look to the world for any example of expression or way of life. If it is a thing of the world, let us not want any part of it! Our minds are renewed! We have the mind of Christ, *not* the mind of the world. We are above the world, for we have set our affections on things above *not* on things of this earth. Paul urgently begged the Romans,

> *Romans 12:1-2 "I beseech you therefore, brethren, by the mercies of God, that ye present your bodies a living sacrifice, holy, acceptable unto God, which is your reasonable service. And be not conformed to this world: but be ye transformed by the renewing of your mind, that ye may prove what is that good, and acceptable, and perfect, will of God."*

Ezekiel 37:1-14 "The hand of the Lord was upon me, and carried me out in the spirit of the Lord, and set me down in the midst of the valley which was full of bones, And caused me to pass by them round about: and, behold, there were very many in the open valley; and, lo, they were very dry. And he said unto me, Son of man, can these bones live? And I answered, O Lord God, thou knowest. Again he said unto me, Prophesy upon these bones, and say unto them, O ye dry bones, hear the word of the Lord. Thus saith the Lord God unto these bones; Behold, I will cause breath to enter into you, and ye shall live: And I will lay sinews upon you, and will bring up flesh upon you, and cover you with skin, and put breath in you, and ye shall live; and ye shall know that I am the Lord. So I prophesied as I was commanded: and as I prophesied, there was a noise, and behold a shaking, and the bones came together, bone to his bone. And when I beheld, lo, the sinews and the flesh came up upon them, and the skin covered them above: but there was no breath in them. Then said he unto me, Prophesy unto the wind, prophesy, son of man, and say to the wind, Thus saith the Lord God; Come from the four winds, O breath, and breathe upon these slain, that they may live. So I prophesied as he commanded me, and the breath came into them, and they lived, and stood up on their feet, an exceeding great army. Then he said unto me, Son

> *of man, these bones are the whole house of Israel: behold, they say, Our bones are dried, and our hope is lost: we are cut off for our parts. Therefore prophesy and say unto them, Thus saith the Lord God; Behold, O my People, I will open your graves, and cause you to come up out of your graves, and bring you into the land of Israel. And ye shall know that I am the Lord, when I have opened your graves, O my people, and brought you up out of your graves, And shall put my spirit in you, and ye shall live, and I shall place you in your own land: then shall ye know that I the Lord have spoken it, and performed it, saith the Lord."*

God is able to do "exceeding abundantly above" anything that we could even begin to think according to the power that continues to work in "us". If you noticed in the Ezekiel passage, God already planned what He was going to do, but what put His work or acts in motion was when the prophet spoke the words of the Lord! The prophet had to "speak" the Word. The work was not manifested until the prophet "spoke". We must allow the logos Word of God to become Rhema or Breathed Word of God as we breathe the words that bring life into our situation and into our lives. Otherwise, they are merely ink or impressions on a page that bring encouragement to our hearts, minds and our spirits but do nothing for our situations. SPEAK, Man and Woman of God!

We have to let our flesh "die" a graveyard death, so that our spirits will rise with the Spirit of God. God has His plan, but we need to speak His Word into our situations. We need to use transformed tongues and speak with the language of miracles that God has given to us.

You may feel like the situation you are in is your "grave" or might as well be, but don't despair! This situation is so that you can leave your old fleshly mind there, and use the power of your tongue to speak life, allowing yourself to "see" even more of who God is. God will open your grave and reveal Himself to you even more.

"And ye shall know that I am the Lord, when I have opened your graves, O my people, and brought you up out of your graves, And shall put my spirit in you, and ye shall live, and shall place you in your own land:"

> *Isaiah 41:17-18 "When the poor and needy seek water, and there is none, and their tongue faileth for thirst, I the Lord will hear them, I the God of Israel*

> *will not forsake them. I will open rivers in high places, and fountains in the midst of the valleys: I will make the wilderness a pool of water, and the dry land springs of water."*

You will see miracles in the valley! God will open not just one fountain but *fountains* that will burst forth through the land, right in the middle of your valley! Even your wilderness—your *wilderness* will become pools of water! You don't need to be taken away from the dry land and taken to water, for your dry land will *become* springs of water!

When Daniel was shut up in the lion's den, the very beasts that men thought would kill him became his comfort. God transformed his valley! His death valley became a place of rest!

When Hananiah, Mishael, and Azariah (better known as Shadrach, Meshach, and Abednego) were bound with ropes and thrown into the fiery furnace, they were seen walking peacefully *in* the fire with Jesus! God walked into and transformed their valley! Oh, come on and give Him glory!

Let's look at one more passage concerning valley transformation.

Acts 16:25-26 "And at midnight Paul and Silas prayed, and sang praises unto God: and the prisoners heard them. And suddenly there was a great earthquake, so that the foundations of the prison were shaken: and immediately all the doors were opened, and every one's bands were loosed. And the keeper of the prison awaking out of his sleep, and seeing the prison doors open, he drew out his sword, and would have killed himself, supposing that the prisoners had been fled. But Paul cried with a loud voice, saying, Do thyself no harm: for we are all here. Then he called for a light, and sprang in, and came trembling, and fell down before Paul and Silas, And brought them out, and said, Sirs, what must I do to be saved?"

There is so much in this passage of scripture. So much that I am excited while I write!

Here, Paul and Silas were in a "valley", a dark and low place in life. They were imprisoned, because they had delivered a young lady from demonic oppression. That caused her to no longer be in a position to make money for her bosses. The love of money is the root of all evil.

So, the crowd rose against them. They ripped the clothes of Paul and Silas from their bodies and beat them with many stripes. Then, they put them in the inner prison—the dungeon of punishment—more severe than the outer prison, with their feet bound. All of that! Why? Because these prophets had messed with their money. So, they were quite possibly in pain, as well as bound as if they were murderers. The prison was definitely pitch dark at midnight, for when the keeper rushed in, he needed a light to see that all the prisoners were still there. But even when it was so dark they couldn't see who was with them, Paul and Silas prayed. They didn't just pray, but they sang praises unto God! I imagine it was so quiet and hollow in there, that their songs of praise were comforting and encouraging for the other prisoners, as the music echoed in the stillness. *"How shall we sing the LORD's song in a strange land?" Psalm 137:4* Just like this: with confidence, boldness and jubilation. Just do it.

While they sang, God caused the earth to shake and the bands of everyone, not just those of Paul and Silas, but everyone's bands were loosed, and all the doors were opened! The earthquake awakened the keeper who came running in. He saw all the prison doors opened and assumed he was a dead man walking for not securing the prisoners on his watch, so he was about to just go ahead and commit suicide.

He couldn't see the prisoners, but Paul could see him, and saved the keeper's life.

The keeper may not have thought the earthquake to be a miraculous act of God at that time. To him, it was probably just natural seismic activity, causing him trouble, and quite possibly costing him his life. Although earthquakes were not extremely common in the Middle East at that time, they were known to happen. In fact, an earthquake had occurred not long before then, when Christ gave His life on the cross.

For this keeper, the miracle was that these men possessed such honest and strong character that they remained there in the prison, unbound, with doors wide open, and not only that! They had the power to keep all the other prisoners from running away to their own freedom! What kind of men are these? This is powerful! He wanted such character and power.

Studying this chapter further, one will notice just how much this valley was transformed! This entire situation was moved from darkness to light, sin to salvation, prison to freedom, and death to life! That prison was transformed to a place of repentance, forgiveness and salvation! How? Two people held on to faith in God, and refusing to look down at their situation, looked up to God and His purpose in their valley, singing and boldly declaring their faith. They had complete trust in God, and God transformed their valley. Just keep praising. You'll discover the purpose in your valley. Just praise.

LESSON 10

Valley Blessings

Psalm 65:13 "The pastures are clothed with flocks; the valleys also are covered over with corn; they shout for joy, they also sing."

Riding and walking around Israel a few years ago, I realized that there was thicker and plusher growth in the valleys than in any other area. The valleys were full of vegetation. Even here in America, farmers usually grow their crops in the valleys, not on the mountaintops. The shepherd leads his sheep through the valleys where there are green pastures and usually a stream of water.

Photo 16: One of the many valleys near Anchorage, Alaska

One very strong wile or deception of Satan is to suggest negativity when we speak or think of having to go through a valley in our lives, but the reality is when we go for a ride through the valley, we experience a peaceful, beautiful countryside. Let us begin to think more peacefully and positively of our "valleys".

The valley is our growing place, our place of nourishment, where we are in the presence of El Shaddai *"the all nourishing God"*. We need strength to reach the mountaintop, and in our valley is where we will find that strength. Our blessing of plenty is in the valley. If you think you are in the valley too long, just imagine how much strength you are gaining in order to climb even higher the next time.

Enjoy your time with El Shaddai. Maximize on your time in the valley, with our Savior, with our Healer, our Teacher, our Comforter. Take time to enjoy the blessings of the valley and the presence of our Good Shepherd, Jesus Christ.

> *Joshua 10:12-13 "Then spake Joshua to the Lord in the day when the Lord delivered up the Amorites before the children of Israel, and he said in the sight of Israel, Sun, stand thou still upon Gibeon; and thou,*

> *Moon, in the valley of Ajalon. And the sun stood still, and the moon stayed, until the people had avenged themselves upon their enemies."*

In order for the sun to stand still for Joshua in Gibeon, the moon had to cooperate in the valley and be still there for a day, until Joshua had won the battle. The connection is in the valley!

When you find yourself again in the valley, know that you are needed in this valley for a connection! What does God want to tell you? What does God need you to know? How much more are you going to learn about God this time? Where will this connection take you? How long will you get to be in His presence this time? What joy! What a relationship! Father God takes this time to spend closely with you, to teach you, to show Himself strong on your behalf. Lord, I just want to know you!

Glory to God! Go ahead and take a praise break!

LESSON 11

Valley Decisions

Joel 3:14-16 "Multitudes, multitudes in the valley of decision: for the day of the Lord is near in the valley of decision... but the Lord will be the hope of his people, and the strength of the children of Israel."

Multitudes are still trying to decide which way to go. When we're at the crossroads, we can rest assured that we will see the Lord in our circumstances as we make the right decision. We learn to make these decisions as we journey through our valley. This is a growing process, a walk of faith, and we grow day by day.

Which decision will you make? To totally obey God this time or to go the way you've always gone? If you want God to do something different in your life, *you* are going to have to do something different that might even seem odd. But whatever He tells you to do, obey.

Since you are spending that quality time with the Lord in this valley, that special quiet time, listen for Him, then listen to Him. Don't complain about anything. This is of the utmost importance. Do not complain about anything. Give God praise and glory. *Psalm 107:8 "Oh that men would praise the Lord for His goodness…"*

Wait on Him. Be patient and rest in Him. Listen while your Lord and Savior is speaking. You cannot make the right decision on your own, but God will lead the way. Trust your Shepherd to lead you.

> *Proverb 3:5-6 "Trust in the Lord with all thine heart; and lean not unto thine own understanding. In all thy ways acknowledge him, and he shall direct thy paths."*

Your flesh is under submission now, right? Your spirit, now totally willing, is being led by the Spirit of God. Follow your Good Shepherd yieldingly and completely. Yield yourself to Abba…Papa. Don't worry that you will make a mistake. You will be in His presence, and you will know His leading. God's sheep know His voice. You will know.

LESSON 12

Rest in the Valley

Isaiah 65:10 "And Sharon shall be a fold of flocks, and the valley of Achor a place for the herds to lie down in, for my people that have sought me."

The valley of Achor symbolized the simple state of contentment and peace of the Messianic age. Today should be a better day than yesterday with all the technology and a longer life span, but the *value* of life seems to be decreasing.

The elderly are living longer, but more of them want to die and so some of them commit suicide or request the help of others. Why? Because in living longer, they are longer in their pain, which is often as emotional as it is physical. They have no desire to "be a burden" on anyone, and sometimes they have no close relatives to really care.

More marriages are failing than ever before in our American history. There are more babies born to unwed mothers. Suicide rates among our youth, our men and our women are steadily increasing, holding status as the 3rd leading cause of death among our youth. Homicide continues to increase, and America has lost the so-called "War on Drugs". Drug money has become a part of the economy.

Pastors and churches are constantly in the news for heinous crimes. Reports of pastors committing embezzlement, various sexual crimes, and even murder have become quite common. There is so much fighting, and there are so many disagreements within the churches, that not even church is a safe haven of rest for some people. However, God still promises peace for His people, the greatest peace—the peace that is found right in the middle of the storm. God's answer and promise found in Isaiah 26:3-4 is, Is *"[I] will keep him in perfect peace whose mind is stayed on [me]: because he trusteth in [me]. Trust ye in the Lord forever: for in the Lord Jehovah is everlasting strength:"*

Even in the midst of turmoil we can find a hiding place in our Lord, for He *is* our hiding place. His promise of *perfect* peace and protection are so sure that we can lie down in green pastures, while He restores our souls.

Can you see that picture? Imagine a huge, beautiful, green pasture stretching for as far as the eye can see, beautiful rays of sun with the fresh air of early morning, while somewhere in the background ripples a stream of water. Now, imagine yourself lying anywhere in that big, beautiful pasture, peacefully resting, and as you rest, Jesus sits nearby completely restoring your soul in a way that only He can. The wonderful thing is that this is not just an imagination. This is *real!*

Photo 17: The Jezreel Valley in Israel taken from Mt. Carmel

LESSON 13

Your Place of Refuge

Zechariah 14:5-8 "And ye shall flee to the valley of the mountains; for the valley of the mountains shall reach unto Azal: yea, ye shall flee, like as ye fled from before the earthquake in the days of Uzziah king of Judah: and the Lord my God shall come, and all the saints with thee... And it shall be in that day, that living waters shall go out from Jerusalem..."

Do you ever feel like you just want to run away? Do you ever just want to get away from it all? My get-away place of rest, relaxation and peaceful solace with God is an isolated beach. Maybe you long to embark upon a plane and fly to a remote island or just walk out of the building and keep on walking, never stopping until you get there. Where? You don't even know. You just want to walk until you get "there". Maybe you just want to lie down to a peaceful, resting sleep and never have to awaken to life as it is. Your valley—this situation—can be your place of refuge.

Regardless to your spiritual status, position, title, talent, popularity, gifts--and sometimes *because* of these high places, these mountainous positions, these pedestals upon which people place you, you may go through a hurtful, disappointing, lonely, rough experience, never seeming to get out of it. Don't worry about your present situation. Don't focus on the situation. Allow God to do whatever needs to be done concerning you, while you're in your valley. This is your time to stop. This is your place of refuge. This is your hiding place. Try to enjoy it. This is your individual, unique, special time with God.

Our lives and minds are always so busy, and when everything is going well, sometimes we don't spend time with God. Sometimes, we don't spend quality time in prayer with God, until we are in a low place. So, to receive what we need from God, to commune with Him, which is His will more than it is your desire, we need the valley experiences. Our Father God longs to talk with us.

Remember when Jezebel was seeking to kill Elijah, and Elijah had that famous competition with the prophets of Baal on Mt. Carmel? Of course, God won, and Elijah had the prophets of Baal killed, but right afterwards, because Elijah was tired of running for his life, he sat under a juniper tree and requested to die. God had *just* used him to show everyone that God is the only God! God had just performed a great miracle through Elijah! Yet, he sought refuge in death. His words were, *1 Kings 19:4 "It is enough; now, O Lord, take away my life; ..."*

While there, God sent one of His tens of thousands of angels to feed and minister to Elijah. While you are in your place of refuge, while you are in the position of wanting to just leave and get away, now in this place... living waters shall go out from Jerusalem. God will send the morning dew from Heaven, and you will feel, time after time, the brush of angels' wings. You will feel God refreshing you. Receive this refreshing. It is your valley, but it is a place of refuge, a place for God's refreshing and restoration. Receive all God wants to give you.

Photo 18: A valley in Oman

Photo 19: Taken in a valley in Oman

LESSON 14

A Place of Nourishment

The Lord's name, *El Shaddai*, is believed to be derived from the Hebrew term *shad* which is a nursing mother's breast. The nourishment from a mother's breasts is all that a baby needs to be fully and completely satisfied, filled and nourished. The child is close to the warmth of the mother, being protected by her, and fed completely by the milk from her breast. El Shaddai, our *only* God, is all-sufficient, all mighty to supply and nourish, and He offers us complete nourishment. God is with us in all valleys as El Shaddai. Even in the valley, He is *all* that we need.

> *Psalm 84:5-7 "Blessed is the man whose strength is in thee; in whose heart are the ways of them. Who passing through the valley of Baca make it a well; the rain also filleth the pools. They go from strength to strength, every one of them in Zion appeareth before God."*

Isn't that powerful? Just passing through the valley, it becomes a well! There are pools—not just streams or holes, but pools *filled* with rain! My God! Many pools filled with rain are made there in the valley *just for you!* Don't despise the rain. There is a purpose for the rain! The rain will sustain you!

This is not the time for giving up or holding your head down, but now is when you go from strength to strength. You are strong when you go into the valley. That's why God often leads you into a fast or a time of consecration just before your valley begins. See, He always knows what's ahead, because the plan is His. If you're obeying Him, then you are fulfilling and carrying out His plan that He created. So, He makes sure that you are strong when you enter the valley, just so that you can be even stronger when you move from your valley to the mountaintop!

You don't use up all of your strength going through the valley. You gain strength as you are nourished and as you walk with Jesus. And with every step, there is more—you go from strength to strength. Did you get that? You go from strength to strength! *From* strength *to* strength!

> *Deuteronomy 1:24-25 "And they turned and went up into the mountain, and came unto the valley of Eshcol, and searched it out. And they took of the fruit of the land in their hands, and brought it down unto us, and brought us word again, and said, It is a good land which the Lord our God doth give us."*
>
> *Genesis 26:19 "And Isaac's servants digged in the valley, and found there a well of springing water."*

Have you "digged" in your valley to see what you can find? Have you searched and stayed before the Lord to see what exactly is in your valley? Strength? A well of springing water? Good fruit? Healing? Deliverance? A Business? Restoration? Financial miracles? Marriage? Family? Wisdom? Or have you just complained and sorrowed over the valley without realizing that God is there, too, and this is all part of His plan for you? The well of springing water—it's in the valley!

The word "baca" means "weeping", so the Valley of Baca is the Valley of Weeping. During your times of weeping, your tears should be turned into a well. Use them for the glory of God. When you get through your weeping, share your testimony with others. Be a testimony. Be a light for those who are in the valley that you've already gone through. Let your tears be the well for someone else to drink and draw strength from. Give God the glory!

The rain is needed for nourishment and growth. Don't cry and complain because of the rain. Benefit from the rain! Grow! Become stronger! Pause to rest, but don't stop. Keep moving. Go from strength to strength!

Unbelievers often get depressed or anxious and turn to alcohol, drugs, suicide, or other means, but not saints of Jehovah! Children of Elohim use their spiritual eyes. Citizens of God's Kingdom walk by faith! We see the next mountain, the level of which just may be determined by the level of the valley! The lower the valley, the higher the mountains seem when you look up to them. *What's ahead for you? Are you ready?*

Letter of Encouragement

****

Dear Saint of the Most High,
The Only Living God, Our Father,

No matter what… open your mouth and really praise God! Praise will change your atmosphere, your day, your situation, your life! Praise will put you in position to do the work of Christ. Praise will defeat doubt. Praise will conquer fear. There is promotion in praise! There is promotion through praise! We are promoted to praise even more! Praise will show others the power and glory of God. The power of God needs to be seen through our lives, so we need to usher victory and power into our lives.

Let us no longer allow circumstances and situations to control our emotions and behavior. We must mount up with wings like eagles and rise above the clouds. We must develop our hind's feet to swiftly move us to high places, after being in the valley for a time getting all that we need for our journey. We must run and not be weary. We must walk and not faint. We must live this life according to God's way, and not write our own rules as we go.

Dr. Arlene Kearns Dowdy

The plan has already been etched with blood. There's no need to shed more blood, etching out another plan. The price has been paid with the blood of an innocent man, our Savior Jesus Christ.

We have many reasons to celebrate and to praise. Praise will work for you, when you don't know what else to do. Let's live God's way, and mount up with God's anointing and power! So, no matter what… PRAISE! Find your YET praise, and PRAISE! Come on up! Come on out! PRAISE! Rejoice! Celebrate Jesus Christ!

With Love,

Your Fellow Servant of Jesus Christ

Web Sources for Bible Study

http://biblehub.com/

http://www.blueletterbible.org/

http://www.truthnet.org

http://www.bible-knowledge.com/

http://www.crosswalk.com/

Photo 20: A natural well in Oman

www.ingramcontent.com/pod-product-compliance
Lightning Source LLC
Chambersburg PA
CBHW060601100426
42744CB00008B/1264